OK OF

nder Hamilton

by DAVID A. ADLER
illustrated by MATT COLLINS

HOLIDAY HOUSE
New York

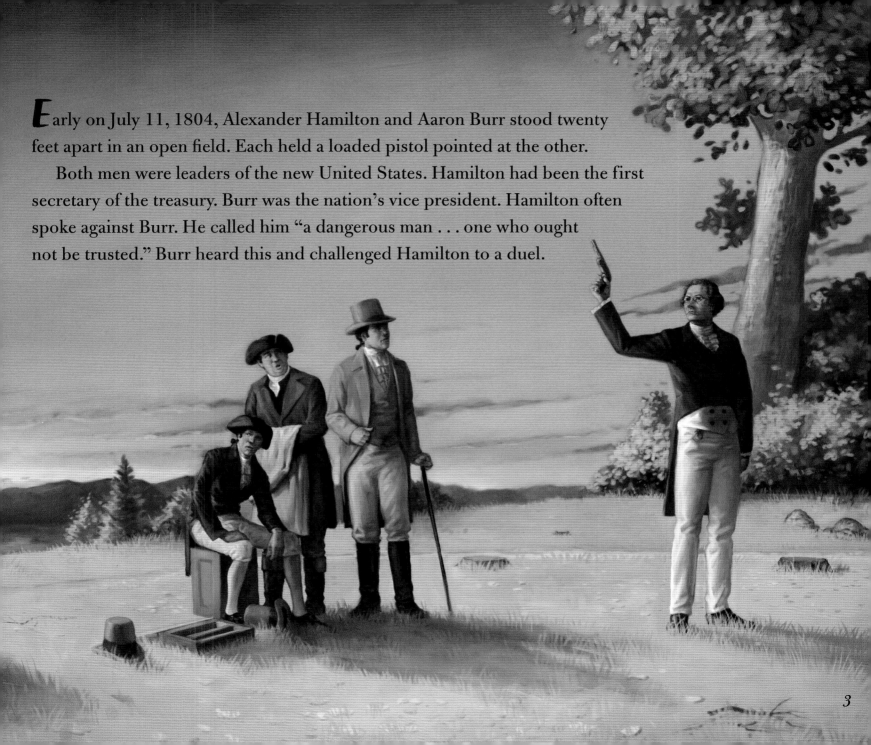

Early on July 11, 1804, Alexander Hamilton and Aaron Burr stood twenty feet apart in an open field. Each held a loaded pistol pointed at the other.

Both men were leaders of the new United States. Hamilton had been the first secretary of the treasury. Burr was the nation's vice president. Hamilton often spoke against Burr. He called him "a dangerous man . . . one who ought not be trusted." Burr heard this and challenged Hamilton to a duel.

4

For Alexander Hamilton it was a long journey to this open field. He was probably born almost fifty years earlier on January 11, 1755, in Nevis, a small Caribbean island with white sand beaches. In the hills were mango, orange, and lemon trees. However, it also had sugar cane plantations worked by enslaved people who had been kidnapped from Africa. Surely Hamilton had witnessed slave auctions and beatings. Later he tried to outlaw slavery in the United States.

Hamilton's mother was the "beautiful and talented" Rachel Faucette. His father was James Hamilton, a failed trader. "My father's affairs at a very early age," Alexander later wrote, "went to wreck."

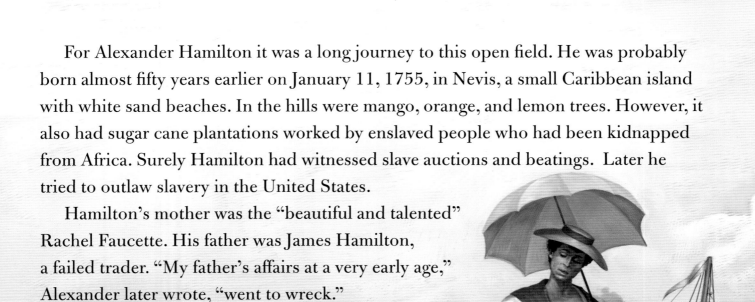

In the early 1750s, after Rachel and James met, she left her husband and son to live with Hamilton. She had several children with him, but only two survived: James Jr. and Alexander. As a child, Alexander was small with reddish-brown hair, blue eyes, and rosy cheeks. His parents were poor. They weren't married.

Their children weren't allowed in most schools, but a small Jewish school welcomed Alexander. There he learned to recite the Ten Commandments in Hebrew.

In April 1765, Alexander's father went to St. Croix, a nearby island, to collect a debt. He took along Rachel and their two sons. But he soon abandoned his family. Alexander never saw him again.

Rachel was left to raise her two sons alone. She opened a small store and sold cloth, meats, dried fish, and rice to the nearby sugar plantations. It wasn't open long.

In early 1768, Rachel became terribly ill, possibly with yellow fever. Soon Alexander was also sick. Rachel Faucette Lavien died on February 19, 1768. Alexander recovered.

At the time, Alexander's brother, James, was working for a carpenter. He moved in with his family. Alexander was taken to live with Ann and Thomas Stevens and their five children. Their son Edward was a year older than Alexander. The two boys became lifelong friends.

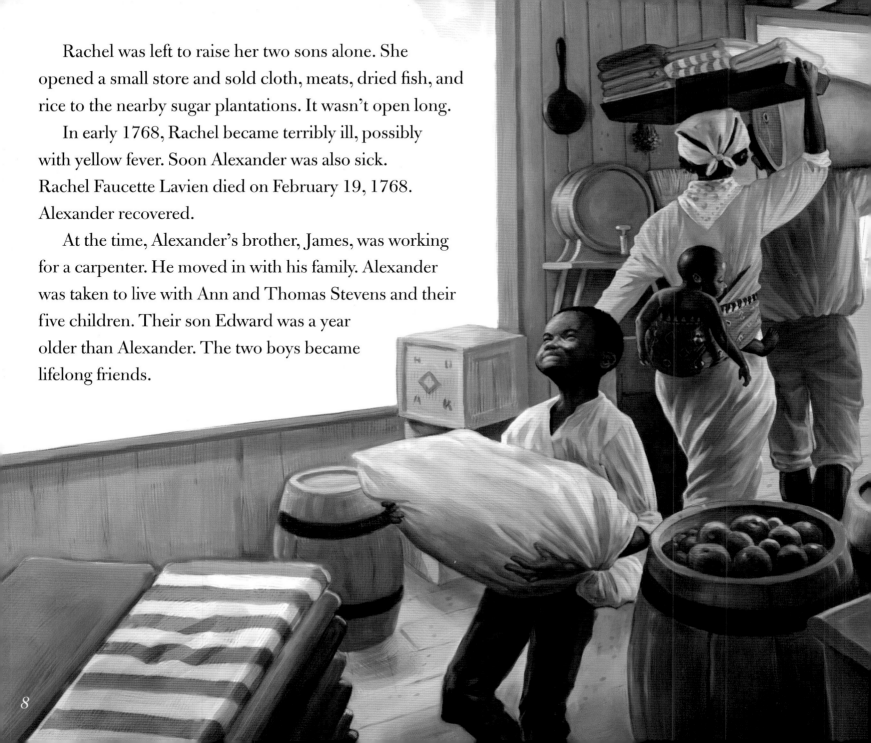

Alexander went to work for Nicholas Cruger, a trader
who had supplied his mother's store. Cruger's company
had offices in several cities including London and New York.
Among the many things they traded were rice, pork, lumber, mules,
and enslaved people. They dealt with the currency of many countries.
Alexander began as a clerk in the St. Croix office.

In 1771, Cruger became ill and traveled to New York for medical
treatment. Sixteen-year-old Alexander was left in charge.

Hamilton supervised ship captains, traded all sorts of goods,
collected money owed the company, and kept careful records of it all.
Four months later, when Cruger returned, he found his business
in good shape.

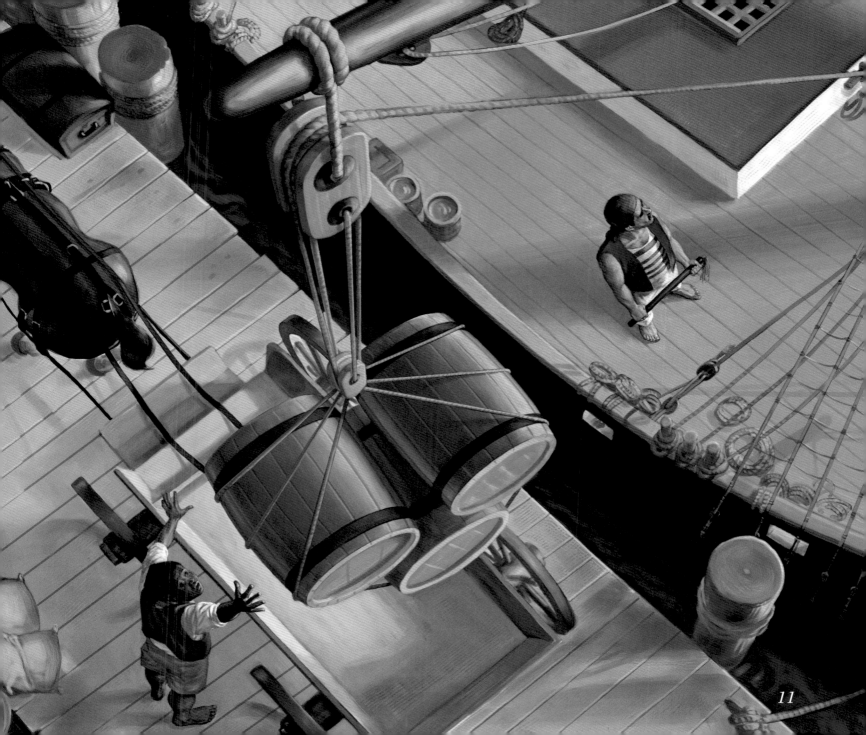

That same year, Reverend Hugh Knox came to St. Croix. He became the pastor of the local church with plans to educate the local "drunkards, gamesters" and "Sabbath breakers." Knox was a powerful speaker with a strong influence on young Hamilton. After reading an essay Hamilton wrote in 1772, Knox would change Hamilton's life.

A mighty hurricane hit the island. "Good God! What horror and destruction," Hamilton wrote. "The roaring of the sea and wind . . . perpetual lightning, the crash of falling houses, the ear-piercing shrieks of the distressed . . . whole families running about the streets."

Knox had Hamilton's descriptive essay published in the local newspaper. People throughout the island read and talked about it. Knox didn't want the brilliant author of this letter to waste away in St.Croix. He raised money and sent Hamilton to college in the American Colonies.

Hamilton studied first with a tutor in Elizabethtown, New Jersey. In 1773, he began his studies at King's College, now called Columbia University, in New York City.

These were difficult times in the American Colonies. They were ruled by Britain, which expected them to pay taxes on many imported products, including tea. In December 1773, to protest, a large group of Boston citizens threw 342 chests of tea into the harbor. This became known as the "Boston Tea Party." In April 1774, two British ships brought tea to New York harbor where American patriots boarded one and threw the tea overboard. The second ship quickly returned to Britain. The colonies were headed toward revolution.

Alexander Hamilton took the side of the American rebels. Over the next two years he wrote long essays in support of the patriots, but he didn't sign his name to them. Someone suggested to Myles Cooper, the president of King's College, that his student had written the essays, but Cooper refused to believe that "so young a man" as Hamilton could have written such strong words.

On April 19, 1775, shots were fired in Concord, Massachusetts—the first shots of the American Revolution. The patriots formed the Continental Army led by George Washington.

Hamilton hoped to fight for the new nation. He and some other students got together each morning in a nearby churchyard and practiced marching, loading muskets, and aiming their guns. They wore green coats and leather hats.

In March 1776, Hamilton was appointed a captain in the Continental Army. But he had to raise his own troop of thirty men. He got more than sixty. He insisted on strict discipline. He made sure they looked like soldiers too. He gave them blue coats with brass buttons and leather pants. His men fought bravely in two New Jersey battles. In late October 1776, in White Plains, New York, Hamilton's men fought alongside Washington's.

In January 1777, Hamilton joined Washington's staff. He was now a lieutenant colonel.

While working with Washington, Hamilton met the leaders of the new nation—members of the Continental Congress. He saw problems in the loose union of the original thirteen states. He thought the central government was too weak to survive.

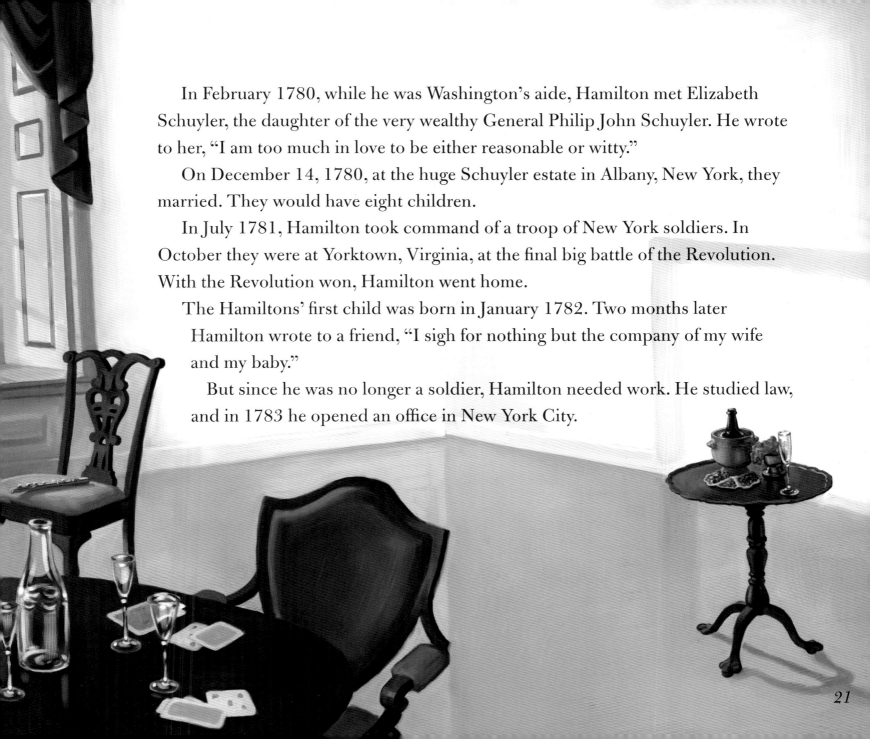

In February 1780, while he was Washington's aide, Hamilton met Elizabeth Schuyler, the daughter of the very wealthy General Philip John Schuyler. He wrote to her, "I am too much in love to be either reasonable or witty."

On December 14, 1780, at the huge Schuyler estate in Albany, New York, they married. They would have eight children.

In July 1781, Hamilton took command of a troop of New York soldiers. In October they were at Yorktown, Virginia, at the final big battle of the Revolution. With the Revolution won, Hamilton went home.

The Hamiltons' first child was born in January 1782. Two months later Hamilton wrote to a friend, "I sigh for nothing but the company of my wife and my baby."

But since he was no longer a soldier, Hamilton needed work. He studied law, and in 1783 he opened an office in New York City.

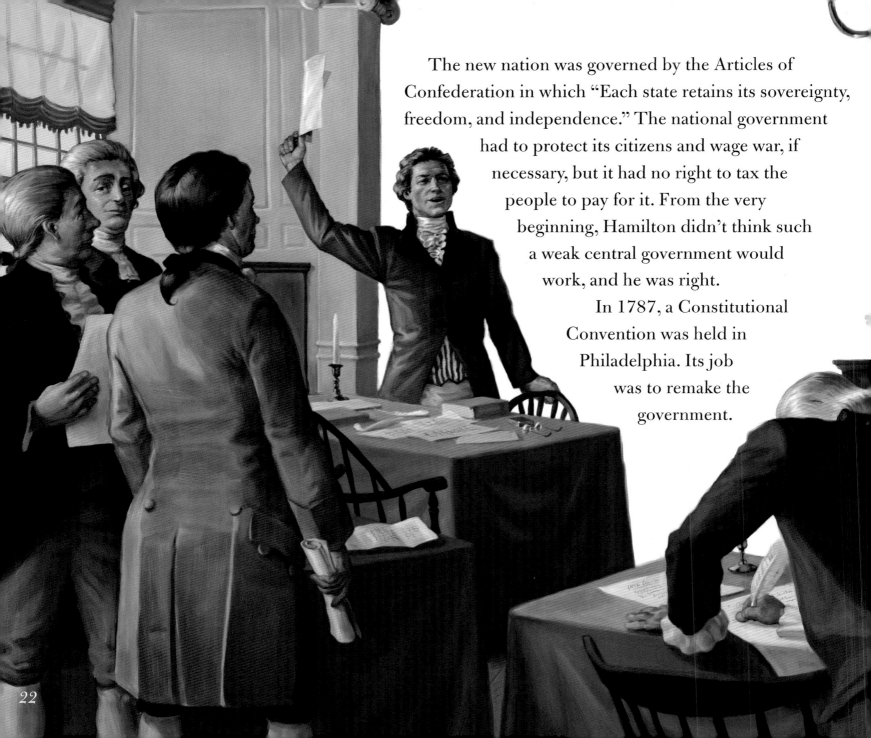

The new nation was governed by the Articles of Confederation in which "Each state retains its sovereignty, freedom, and independence." The national government had to protect its citizens and wage war, if necessary, but it had no right to tax the people to pay for it. From the very beginning, Hamilton didn't think such a weak central government would work, and he was right.

In 1787, a Constitutional Convention was held in Philadelphia. Its job was to remake the government.

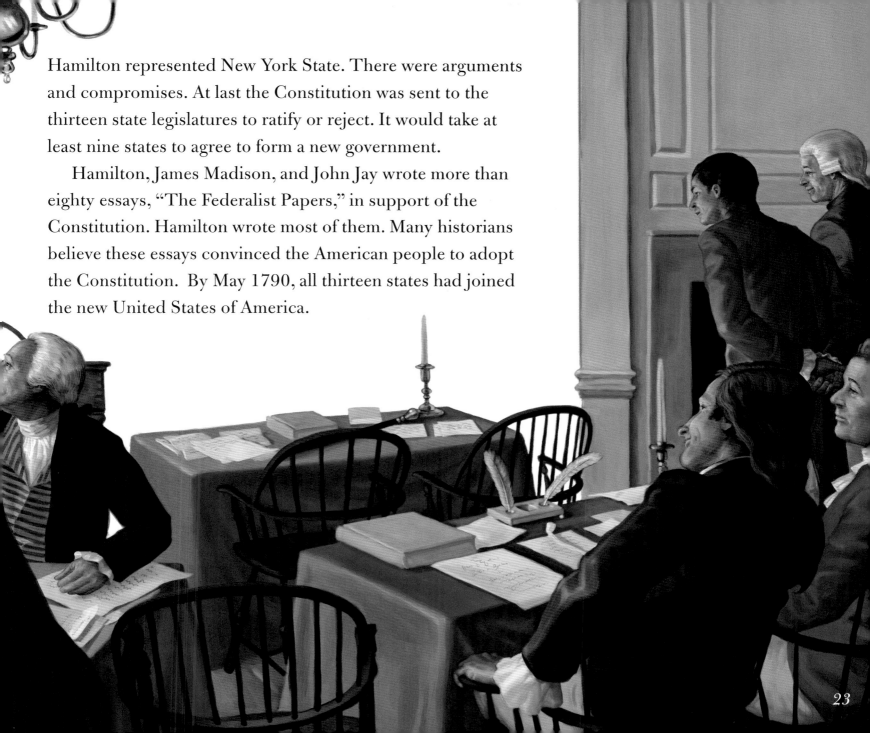

Hamilton represented New York State. There were arguments and compromises. At last the Constitution was sent to the thirteen state legislatures to ratify or reject. It would take at least nine states to agree to form a new government.

Hamilton, James Madison, and John Jay wrote more than eighty essays, "The Federalist Papers," in support of the Constitution. Hamilton wrote most of them. Many historians believe these essays convinced the American people to adopt the Constitution.  By May 1790, all thirteen states had joined the new United States of America.

The Constitution called for a president to lead the nation. The nation's founders chose George Washington. He needed people to help him govern—a cabinet—and chose Hamilton to be his secretary of the treasury.

Hamilton set up a national bank to collect taxes, borrow money, pay for an army, and control trade between states and other countries. His bank became our Federal Reserve System, which today plays an important role in running our economy.

When Hamilton took office, people in the United States still used British currency. He proposed having a new national currency. The coins would be as small as a penny and a half-penny. Even poor people could have and spend it.

Hamilton's taxes were not popular. In September 1791, farmers in Pennsylvania covered a tax agent with hot tar and feathers to protest the tax on whiskey. In July 1794, someone set fire to a tax collector's home. Hamilton convinced President Washington that the country's laws must be obeyed.

Troops were sent to end what has been called the "Whiskey Rebellion."

Some people approved of Hamilton enforcing the nation's laws. Others felt Hamilton was creating a too-powerful federal government. This led to the formation of two political parties. Hamilton's Federalist Party wanted a strong central government. Thomas Jefferson's Democratic-Republican Party wanted more control left to the states. The 1796 election for the president to succeed Washington was the first with two candidates, each supported by a different political party.

Hamilton and Burr were political enemies belonging to opposing parties. Hamilton was a Federalist and Burr a Democratic-Republican. Hamilton said of Burr, "He cares only for himself, and nothing for his country or glory. . . . He has but one principle—to get power by any means, and to keep it by all means."

They had their duel on July 11, 1804. Hamilton was shot, and died the next day. Two days later he was buried. Church bells tolled in his memory. Cannons were fired. People crowded the streets of New York City to watch the funeral procession. They looked from their windows. They stood on rooftops. The nation had lost one of its most important Founding Fathers.

# Important Dates in the Life of Alexander Hamilton

1755   Legal documents of the time give 1755 as the year of his birth. Hamilton claimed he was born on January 11, 1757.

1765   His father, James Hamilton, left his wife and two sons.

1768   His mother became ill with high fever. She died February 19.

1771   For four months he managed his boss's complicated trading business.

1772   Traveled to the American Colonies for schooling.

1773   Began study at King's College in New York City.

1776   Appointed captain of a New York regiment in the Continental Army.

1777   Became an aide to General George Washington.

1780   Married Elizabeth Schuyler on December 14.

1782   Studied law and was admitted to plead before the New York State Supreme Court.

1786   Elected member of the New York State Assembly.

1801   Eldest child Philip shot in a duel on November 23. He died the next day.

1804   Wrote that Aaron Burr, who was seeking election as Governor of New York, was "a dangerous man." Burr challenged Hamilton to a duel. Hamilton was shot on July 11 and died the next day.

# Selected Bibliography

Brookhiser, Richard. *Alexander Hamilton, American*. New York: The Free Press, 1999.

Chernow, Ron. *Alexander Hamilton*. New York: Penguin, 2004.

Emery, Noemie. *Alexander Hamilton: An Intimate Portrait*. New York: Putnam, 1982.

Freeman, Joanne, ed. *Alexander Hamilton: Writings*. New York: Library of America, 1979.

Hall, Margaret Esther. *Alexander Hamilton Reader: A Compilation of Materials By, and Commenting on, Hamilton*. New York: Oceana, 1957.

Kline, Mary-Jo. *Alexander Hamilton: A Biography in His Own Words*. New York: Newsweek, 1973.

McDonald, Forrest. *Alexander Hamilton: A Biography*. New York: W.W. Norton, 1979.

Miller, John C. *Alexander Hamilton: Portrait in Paradox*. New York: Barnes and Noble, 1959.

Randall, Willard Sterne. *Alexander Hamilton: A Life*. New York: Harper Collins, 2003.

# Notes

Alexander Hamilton was said to have a strong physical resemblance to his friend Edward Stevens, which has made some people speculate that they were half brothers. That might explain why Thomas Stevens was willing to take in Alexander and but not his brother James.

Hugh Knox studied at the College of New Jersey, later called Princeton University. At the time of his study the president of the college was Aaron Burr, the father of the future vice president, the man who would kill Alexander Hamilton.

Hamilton's eldest child Philip died in a duel in 1801. The next year the Hamiltons' eighth child was born and was also named Philip. There has been an occasional miscount of the number of the Hamiltons' children, because they had two sons with the same name.

p. 3 "a dangerous man . . . not be trusted." Chernow, p. 680.

p. 5 "Beautiful and talented," Chernow, p. 16.

p. 5 "My father's affairs . . . went to wreck." Freeman, p. 880.

p. 13 "drunkards, gamesters" and "Sabbath breakers." Chernow, p. 35.

p. 13 "Good God! . . . running about the streets." Hall, pp. 33–34.

p. 17 "so young a man," Chernow, p. 61.

p. 21 "I am too much . . . reasonable or witty." Miller, pp. 64–65.

p. 21 "I sign for . . . and my baby." Kline, p. 115.

p. 29 "He cares . . . by all means," Hall, pp. 229–230.

p. 30 "a dangerous man." Freeman, p. 1051.

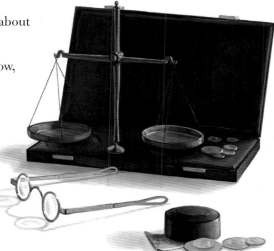

*For Arlene and Joseph —D. A. A.*

*For Fox Taconic Watson —M. C.*

Text copyright © 2019 by David A. Adler • Illustrations copyright © 2019 by Matt Collins • All Rights Reserved
HOLIDAY HOUSE is registered in the U.S. Patent and Trademark Office. • Printed and bound in May 2020 at Tien Wah Press, Johor Bahru, Johor, Malaysia.
The artwork was created with using Prismacolor pencils and Painter 12.2.1.
www.holidayhouse.com • First Edition • 3 5 7 9 10 8 6 4 2

Library of Congress Cataloging-in-Publication Data • Names: Adler, David A., author. | Collins, Matt, illustrator.
Title: A picture book of Alexander Hamilton / by David A. Adler ; illustrated by Matt Collins. • Description: First edition.
New York : Holiday House, 2019. Includes bibliographical references. • Identifiers: LCCN 2019005694 | ISBN 9780823439614 (hardcover)
Subjects: LCSH: Hamilton, Alexander, 1757–1804—Juvenile literature. Statesmen—United States—Biography—Juvenile literature. | United States—
Politics and government—1783–1809—Juvenile literature. Classification: LCC E302.6.H2 A17 2019 | DDC 973.4092 [B]—dc23
LC record available at https://lccn.loc.gov/2019005694 | ISBN 9780823447275 (paperback)